My Weird School
FAST FACTS
Dogs, Cats, and Dung Beetles

Also by Dan Gutman

My Weird School

My Weird School Daze

My Weirder School

My Weirdest School

My Weird School Fast Facts

The Baseball Card Adventure series

The Genius Files

The Flashback Four series

Rappy the Raptor

Johnny Hangtime

My Weird School FAST FACTS
Dogs, Cats, and Dung Beetles

Dan Gutman
Pictures by
Jim Paillot

HARPER
An Imprint of HarperCollinsPublishers

To Nina

The author gratefully acknowledges the editorial contributions of Nina Wallace.

Photograph credits: Page 6: Bildagentur Zoonar GmbH / Shutterstock; Page 8: Ricantimages / Shutterstock; Page 13: Bill Greene / The Boston Globe via Getty Images; Page 17: KateSun / Shutterstock; Page 25: AP Photo / Mark Thiessen; Page 30: insima / Shutterstock; Page 32: Public Domain; Page 34: Henk Vrieselaar / Shutterstock; Page 35: Public Domain; Page 39: Procy / Shutterstock; Page 41: Pascale Gueret / Shutterstock; Page 45: Keneva Photography / Shutterstock; Page 51: Bryan Busovicki / Shutterstock; Page 58: zaferkizilkaya / Shutterstock; Page 64: Lara Zanarini / Shutterstock; Page 66: Patrick K. Campbell / Shutterstock; Page 73: Gerald Robert Fischer / Shutterstock; Page 79: Jordan Adkins / Shutterstock; Page 83: reptiles4all / Shutterstock; Page 88: Schnapps2012 / Shutterstock; Page 101: Jaime Chavez / Shutterstock; Page 108: Paul Looyen / Shutterstock; Page 112: Chanwit Polpakdee / Shutterstock; Page 125: Edmund Lowe Photography / Shutterstock; Page 131: JOHANNES EISELE/AFP/Getty Images; Page 147: Universal History Archive/UIG via Getty Images; Page 152: NASA; Page 159: MZPHOTO.CZ / Shutterstock; Page 168: gary powell / Shutterstock; Page 175: Vladimir Wrangel / Shutterstock

ISBN 978-0-06-267306-0 (pbk. bdg.)–ISBN 978-0-06-267307-7 (library bdg.)

20 21 22 BRR 10 9 8 7 6 5
❖
First Edition

Contents

The Beginning

My name is Professor A.J., and I know everything there is to know about animals. The first thing you need to know about animals is this—animals are weird.

You don't believe me? Maybe a few fast facts will convince you. . . .

When some snails lose an eye, they can grow a new one!

Leopard seals don't have ears on their head!

Penguins have knees!

Octopuses have nine brains and three hearts!

Crocodiles can't stick out their tongues!

A starving mouse will eat its own tail!

Manatees swim by farting!

 Wait a minute! We're not going to talk about farting and disgusting things like that in this book. Remember we talked about that?

Oh no! It's Andrea Young, that annoying girl in my class with curly brown hair! Who invited *you* into my book, Andrea?

It's *our* book, Arlo!* It's not *your* book. We're supposed to talk about animals *together.* Remember? This is our special project for the gifted and talented program.

Bummer in the summer! Why can't a truck full of gifted and talented animals fall on your head? Okay,

*Andrea calls me by my real name because she knows I don't like it. She is annoying.

3

okay. I'll hold my tongue. See? I'm holding my tongue! But sit back and enjoy the weirdest, wackiest fast facts about animals in the history of the world.

Sincerely,

Professor A.J.

(The Professor of Awesomeness)

The Professor of Obnoxiousness is more like it! Don't worry. I won't let Arlo talk about gross stuff and things that are inappropriate for children. *Somebody's* got to be mature around here.

Andrea Young, PhD

(I'm going to Harvard someday.)

Chapter 1

Dogs

 We should start with dogs because lots of kids have dogs, and dogs are cool. Did you know that dogs have nose prints just like people have fingerprints! You can even identify your dog by its nose print.

 French poodles didn't come

from France. They came from Germany.

Dalmatians aren't born with spots. They're completely white at birth. The spots start to show up when they're about ten days old.

The shoulder blades on a dog are not tightly attached to the rest of its skeleton. That makes it easier for a dog to run.

Do you know why male dogs raise their leg while peeing on a tree? They want other dogs to think they're bigger. Some wild dogs in Africa even run up tree trunks while they're peeing.

 No pee facts, Arlo! We talked about this!

Okay, okay! The oldest dog in the history of the world was an Australian cattle dog named Bluey. He lived almost thirty years, from 1910 to 1939.

The smallest dog ever was a Yorkshire terrier. It was less than three inches tall and less than four inches from nose to tail, and it weighed only four ounces. It must have been adorable!

 The biggest dog in the history of the world was Zorba, an English mastiff. He weighed 343 pounds and was eight feet three inches from the tip of his nose to the tip of his tail.

An English mastiff

You may have heard that you should never feed chocolate

to a dog. Here are some other foods that might make your dog sick: macadamia nuts, corn on the cob, grapes, raisins, onions, tobacco, or anything with caffeine.

When the famous ship the *Titanic* sank, three of the survivors were dogs. Two of them were

Pomeranians; the third was a Pekinese. They were all small dogs, so probably nobody noticed when they were carried onto the lifeboats.

 Dogs can see in the dark, and they have three eyelids on each eye!

 When dogs sweat, it comes out the pads of their feet.

 We have about nine thousand taste buds. Dogs have less than two thousand. But don't feel bad for dogs. Their sense of smell is ten *thousand* times stronger than ours.

 In 2015, lampposts were falling down in San Diego. You'll never believe why. Dogs were peeing on them, and a chemical in the urine was rotting the metal! Also, when dogs poop, they like to choose their direction based on the Earth's magnetic field!

 Arlo! What did we say about peeing and pooping?

 Okay, okay! The Norwegian Lundehund is the only dog that has six toes on each foot.

A Great Pyrenees named Duke has been the mayor of

Cormorant, Minnesota, for three consec-
utive terms.

 A German shepherd named
Orient walked over two

thousand miles on the Appalachian Trail. The really amazing part is that Orient was a seeing-eye dog, and his owner, Bill Irwin, was the first blind man to make that trip.

Bill Irwin and Orient

 In 2013, a service dog named Kirsch got an honorary master's degree from Johns Hopkins University. Kirsch got it because he attended all his owner's classes. He even wore a cap and gown for the ceremony.

There are more dogs in the

United States than in any other country in the world. But in Iran, owning a dog is against the law.

 In the song "A Day in the Life," the Beatles included a whistle that only dogs can hear.

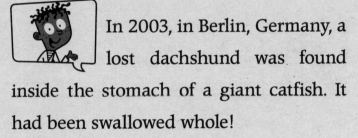 In 2003, in Berlin, Germany, a lost dachshund was found inside the stomach of a giant catfish. It had been swallowed whole!

By the way, do you know what you call a fish that's missing an eye?*

---

*A fsh

A British scientist invented the "wag-o-meter," a machine that indicated a dog's mood by the way it wagged its tail. The machine was attached to the back of a dog, and it measured the speed and direction of the wagging. Side-to-side wagging meant the dog was happy. When the tail went straight up with just a tiny wag at the tip, that meant the dog was about to attack.

Speaking of dog machines, back in 1897, many homes didn't have electricity, so Sears Roebuck sold a "dog power" machine. It was basically a treadmill for dogs that could be connected to any device that required turning, like a butter churn or a washing machine. When the dog walked on the treadmill, it made the machine turn! For big jobs, you could buy a two-dog tread-mill.

When the German countess Karlotta Liebenstein died in 1991, she left eighty *million* dollars to her dog. It's no longer alive, but the dog's son is so rich that he owns villas in Italy and the Bahamas. In 2000, he purchased Madonna's Miami Beach mansion for seven and a half million dollars!

Weird Mixed-Breed Dog Names

Bully Pitsky: American Bully and Siberian or Alaskan husky

Chusky: Chow Chow and Siberian husky

Chug: Pug and Chihuahua

Horgi: Corgi and Siberian husky

A chug

Schnoodle: Schnauzer and poodle

Corgipoo: Poodle and corgi

Corgle: Corgi and beagle

Goberian: Golden retriever and Siberian husky

Frug: French bulldog and pug

Whoodle: Poodle and Wheaten terrier

Bernedoodle: Bernese mountain dog and poodle

• • • •

Barking Around the World

Dogs don't always go *bow-wow* or *woof-woof.* Here's what people say in other languages to describe the sound dogs make. . . .

Afrikaans: *blaf-blaf; woef-woef; keff-keff*

Arabic: *hau-hau; how-how*

Armenian: *haf-haf*

Belgian: *wooah-wooah*

Bulgarian: *bau-bau; jaff-jaff*

Burmese: *woke-woke*

Cantonese: *wo-wo; wow-wow; wong-wong*

Czech: *haff-haff*

Danish: *vov-vov; vuf-vuf*

Dutch: *blaf-blaf; woef-woef*

Finnish: *hau-hau; vuh-vuh; rauf-rauf*

German: *wuff-wuff; vow-vow*

Greek: *ghav-ghav*

Hebrew: *hav-hav; haw-haw-how-how*

Hindi: *bow-bow*

Italian: *bau-bau; arf-arf*

Japanese: *wan-wan; kian-kian*

Korean: *meong-meong; mung-mung; wang-wang*

Mandarin: *wang-wang*

Norwegian: *voff-voff; boff-boff; vov-vov*

Polish: *hau-hau*

Romanian: *ham-ham; hau-hau*

Russian: *gav-gav; guf-guf; hav-hav*

Spanish: *guau-guau; gua-gua; jau-jau*

Swedish: *voff-voff; vov-vov*

Tamazight: *hav-hav; haw-haw*

Thai: *hong-hong*

Turkish: *hev-hev; hav-hav*

Vietnamese: *gau-gau; wau-wau; ang-ang*

By the way, do you know how to stop a dog that's barking in the backseat of your car?*

● ● ● ● ● ● ● ● ● ● ● ● ● ●

Weird Dog Laws

In Oklahoma: Dogs can't gather in groups of three or more on private property unless they have a permit signed by the mayor.

---

*Put it in the front seat.

21

In Normal, Illinois: It's against the law to make faces at dogs.

In Anchorage, Alaska: You can't tie your pet dog to the roof of a car.

In Little Rock, Arkansas: Dogs aren't allowed to bark after six o'clock.

In Hartford, Connecticut: You aren't allowed to educate a dog.

In Chicago, Illinois: It's illegal to give a dog whiskey.

In Galesburg, Illinois: You can't keep a smelly dog.

In North Brook, Illinois: It's against the law for a dog to bark for more than fifteen minutes.

Chapter 2

Cats

You think dogs are the most popular pet in America? Well, you're wrong! We have seventy-four million dogs and eighty-eight million cats. So nah-nah-nah boo-boo on dogs!

Cats are like superheroes. They can jump up to six times

their length! They can hear sounds up to two octaves higher than a human! They can fit through an opening the size of their head! They can drink seawater to survive!

 Did you ever hear that cats always land on their feet? Well, it's true. They have a "righting reflex" that's controlled by the eyes and balance organs in their inner ears. In the 1970s, a cat named Andy fell from the sixteenth floor of an apartment building and survived. Andy was owned by Florida senator Ken Myer.

 In 2013, a cat named Morris ran for mayor of Xalapa, Mexico. It shouldn't be a big surprise that he lost the election. What's surprising is that a cat named Stubbs was the mayor of Talkeetna, Alaska, for fifteen years.

Stubbs the Cat in July 2006

FAT CAT. The heaviest cat in the history of the world was Himmy, from Queensland, Australia. He weighed almost forty-seven pounds! That's a fat cat! No cat will ever beat Himmy because Guinness World Records got rid of this *"cat*egory" (get it?) after

Himmy died in 1986. They were afraid that people would overfeed their cats trying to break the record.

 SKINNY CAT. The lightest cat ever was a blue point Himalayan named Tinker Toy. He weighed just one pound and six ounces. He was less than three inches tall.

 OLD CAT. The oldest cat in the history of the world was Crème Puff, from Austin, Texas. She died in 2005, three days after her thirty-eighth birthday.

RICH CAT. The richest cat ever was named Blackie. His owner was British antique dealer Ben Rea. When Rea died in 1988, Blackie inherited thirteen million dollars.

TIRED CATS. Seventy percent of their lives, cats are sleeping. So a nine-year-old cat has only been awake for three years.*

Cats sort of look like spies, always slinking around and acting mysteriously. Well, in the 1960s, the CIA tried to turn a cat into a *real* spy

---

*And if you think cats are lazy, ferrets sleep about *twenty* hours a day.

by implanting a microphone in its ear canal and a radio transmitter in its chest. Sadly, on its first spy mission, it got hit by a taxi and died.

 Female cats are usually right-handed, I mean, right-pawed. Male cats are usually left-pawed.

Cats have three hundred million neurons in their cerebral cortex. That's the part of the brain that controls information processing. Dogs only have a hundred and sixty million. Does this mean that cats are nearly twice as smart as dogs?

Cats would definitely say so. That is, if they could talk.

 That reminds me, cats can make over a hundred sounds. Dogs can only make ten.

 A cat's heart beats nearly twice as fast as ours—about 140 to 220 beats per minute.

 The ancient Egyptians *loved*  cats, and they even worshipped a cat goddess called Bastet. In 1888, a farmer in Egypt found a tomb filled with eighty thousand cat mummies! When cats died in ancient Egypt, family members would mourn by shaving off their eyebrows.

 Wait. What? Why would they shave off the cat's eyebrows? The ancient Egyptians were weird.

 No, dumbhead! They'd shave off their *own* eyebrows. Cats don't even *have* eyebrows.

 Why would they shave off their own eyebrows just because their cat died?

 How should I know?

 I thought you knew every-thing.

 Famous inventor Nikola Tesla decided to do experiments with electricity after

Nikola Tesla

he observed static electricity on the fur of his cat, Macak.

 You know how they say it's bad luck when a black cat crosses your path? Well, in England and

Australia, black cats are considered to be *good* luck.

 Most cats have between one and nine kittens. But in 1970, a Burmese cat named Tarawood Antigone had nineteen kittens! That's the record.

 Did you know that cats can't taste sugar? It's true. So don't bother putting sugar in their tea.

 Cats are really good at climbing up trees. But they're not so good at climbing *down* trees. That's because their claws curve toward the back. To get down a tree, a cat has to go backward. So if your cat gets stuck in a tree, now you know why.

 A cat's jaw can't move sideways. That's why they can't chew big pieces of food.

 Cats have fifty-three verte- brae.
We humans only have thirty-four.

 Cats have eighteen toes! Well, most of them do anyway. There was this one cat named Jake, from Ontario, Canada, who had twenty-eight toes! That's the most ever, according to Guinness World Records. But who's counting cat toes?

 Did you ever hear of a cat piano? It was supposed to be a musical instrument made out of cats! I kid you not. The "katzenklavier" is credited to a seventeenth-century German scholar named Athanasius Kircher. His idea was that he would find a bunch of cats that had different voice pitches. Then he wanted to put them in a row of cages and "play" his instrument by driving nails into the cats' tails. Okay, that guy

Athanasius Kircher

had problems. Fortunately, his instrument was never actually built, as far as we know.

Did you ever hear somebody say, "It's raining cats and dogs"? That expression may have started from an old poem by Jonathan Swift, describing how heavy rainstorms in England would cause deadly flooding in the streets, so it would look like it had actually rained cats and dogs.

That's pretty depressing, Arlo. I think we should end this chapter with a happier fast fact. People *love* cat videos. In 2015, thirteen thousand people went to the Internet Cat Video Festival in Minnesota. One of the most popular cat videos ever is "Surprised Kitty." I would tell you to watch it, but you probably already did. It's been viewed more than seventy-seven *million* times on YouTube.

Chapter 3

Weird Things Other Animals Do

If you think that dogs and cats are weird, get a load of these *other* animals. They make dogs and cats look *normal*.

A squid's eye can get as big as a basketball!

 Snakes don't blink their eyes!

 A beaver's teeth never stop growing! If a beaver didn't gnaw on stuff all the time, its teeth would grow into its brain.

 Pigs like to play video games that are controlled with a

joystick. Speaking of pigs, Denmark has twice as many pigs as people.

 Hummingbirds are the only birds that can fly backward. Kangaroos can't even *walk* backward.

 During World War II, the United States developed a top-secret program to train bats to drop bombs. It was called Project X-Ray. It would be cool to see a flying bat bomb.

 A goldfish kept in a dark room will lose its color. Its pigment production depends on light. By the way, do you know why fish live in salt water?*

 The flamingo can only eat when its head is upside down.

 Great horned owls have a terrible sense of smell. They're one of the few animals that will eat skunks.

---

*Because pepper makes them sneeze

41

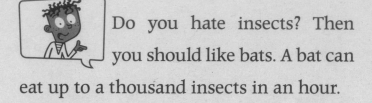

Do you hate insects? Then you should like bats. A bat can eat up to a thousand insects in an hour.

Cows have four stomachs. It's true! And if you play soothing music to a cow, it will produce more milk. By the way, about twenty-two people die each year in the United States because they got trampled by a cow.

Hey, maybe they should have played the cows soothing music!

A hippo's sweat is red—and it doubles as a sunscreen!

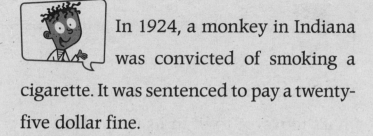 In 1924, a monkey in Indiana was convicted of smoking a cigarette. It was sentenced to pay a twenty-five dollar fine.

 Arlo, do you know how to tell the color of a chicken's eggs?

 By looking at the egg?

Well, yes. That's one way. But you can also look at the chicken's earlobes. A chicken with red earlobes will usually produce brown eggs. A chicken with white earlobes will produce white eggs.

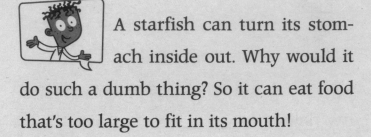 A starfish can turn its stomach inside out. Why would it do such a dumb thing? So it can eat food that's too large to fit in its mouth!

 Also, starfish have eight eyes— one at the end of each arm. And starfish don't have blood. Instead, filtered seawater runs through a starfish.

 Starfish are weird.

A butterfly's taste sensors are on its feet. So it can taste food by standing on it.

 Frogs can't swallow without blinking. And they don't drink water. They absorb it through their skin.

 Sea otters hold hands with each other while they sleep. They do it to keep from drifting apart in the water. That must be adorable!

 Jellyfish are 98 percent water. If you leave them out in the sun too long, they can evaporate!

 Fourteen species of dancing frogs were discovered in 2014. So now there are twenty-four known species of dancing frogs.

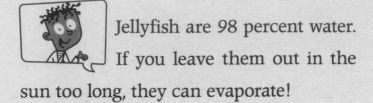 Wait. What? Frogs dance?

Yes, and sea lions can keep a beat. A sea lion named Ronan at the University of California was trained to bob her head to music.

A chameleon's tongue can be twice as long as its body.

Animals can be *loud*. The call of a howler monkey can be heard three miles away. The snapping

shrimp has a claw that creates bubbles that can travel at sixty miles per hour. When the bubble explodes, the sound is louder than a gunshot. And blue whales make low-frequency "pulses" that can be heard five hundred miles away!

Lobsters can detach one of their limbs in an emergency and grow it back during a molting period. I would give my right arm to be able to do that.

Sea horses are the only animals on Earth in which the male gives birth to the babies. Sea horse dads carry fertilized eggs in their pouch and can give birth to more than a thousand babies at a time. Men are so competitive!

Galápagos tortoises can go a year without food or water. Anteaters, on the other hand, eat thirty-five thousand ants a day. And an adult panda spends twelve hours a day eating twenty-eight pounds of bamboo. Yuck!

By the way, do you know why pandas like old movies?*

---

*Because they're in black and white

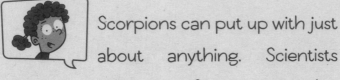 Scorpions can put up with just about anything. Scientists have put scorpions in a freezer overnight, and then in the morning they just walked away—la-di-dah—like nothing had ever happened.

 Why did the scientists walk away from the freezer?

 No, dumbhead! The scientists didn't walk away! The *scorpions* walked away!

 Then why didn't you say so? But do you know how to tell if

a turtle is a boy or a girl? The males grunt and the females hiss.

 I knew that. But did you know that baby giraffes can get up on their feet a half hour after they're born?

 Everybody knows that. But did you know that hippos can hold their breath underwater for as long as five minutes?

Of course I did. But did you know that the black-capped

chickadee gets its name from its call, which sounds like *chickadee-dee-dee*? And when it's in danger, it adds more *dees* to its call.

• • • • • • • • • • • • • • •

Unexpected Flying Animals

Okay, let's get one thing straight. Pigs can't fly. The only animals that can really fly are birds, insects, and bats. But some nutty animals manage to travel through the air by jumping from high places. There are sky-diving ants, leaping lizards, flying frogs, soaring squirrels, and parachuting geckos.

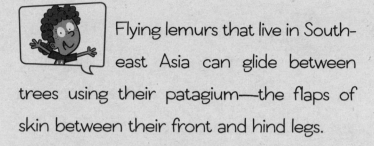 Flying lemurs that live in Southeast Asia can glide between trees using their patagium—the flaps of skin between their front and hind legs.

The feathertail glider is a marsupial the size of a mouse. But it can glide eighty-two feet.

Flying fish can jump out of the water with a push of their pectoral fins. There are about fifty species of fish that can do this, and some have been observed skipping over the waves for as long as forty-five seconds at a time.

 I love penguins. They can jump six feet out of the water. And believe it or not, wild turkeys can soar fifty-five miles per hour—they just can't stay in the air for long.

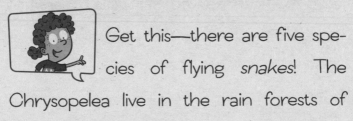 Get this—there are five species of flying *snakes*! The Chrysopelea live in the rain forests of

Southeast Asia. They drop from the tree-tops, flatten their bodies, and move them in an S-shape so wind collects against their skin. They can stay airborne for the length of a bowling lane and deliver a nasty bite.

 Okay, cancel my trip to Southeast Asia.

• • • • • • • • • • • • • • • •

Long Live Animals!

Some animals don't live very long. The gastrotricha is a microscopic aquatic worm. Its average lifespan is only three or four days. And the mayfly is an aquatic insect with an even *shorter* life span. About twenty-four hours after it breaks free from its cocoon, the mayfly's life is over.

 If you ask me, they should call it a may *die*.

On the other hand, some animals live a ridiculously *long* time. Bowhead whales and koi fish can live more than two hundred years. The oldest known fish was named Hanako. She died in 1977 at the age of 226.

I can top that. Tortoises are famous for their long lives. In 2006, in India, a male giant tortoise named

Adwaitya at a zoo in India died at the age of 255. My guess is that he died trying to blow out all the candles on his birthday cake.

 That's nothing. Ming, a deep-sea clam, died in 2006 after living for 507 years. He was killed by accident when scientists in Iceland froze him so they could transport him back to their laboratory.

The Antarctic sponge puts all those animals to shame. It can live over a *thousand* years.

Oh, yeah? Well, what about

the immortal jellyfish? Yes, that's what it's called. These tiny crea- tures can change their

own cells into a different form and grow all over again. So they basically live forever. To infinity and beyond!

I win!

● ● ● ● ● ● ● ● ● ● ● ● ● ● ● ●

False Animal Facts That People Think Are True

Everything else in this book is true. But these "facts" that you may *think* are true are actually false. . . .

• Ostriches bury their heads in the sand.

They don't. Ostriches *are* scaredy-cats that run away or lie on the ground when they're threatened. But they don't bury their heads in the sand.

• Opossums hang by their tails

They don't. They have strong tails, but they're too heavy to hang from them.

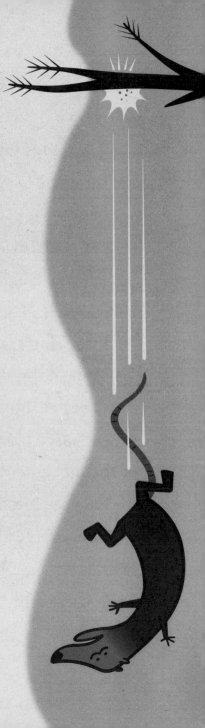

• Touching a toad can give you warts.

It won't.

• Lemmings jump off cliffs as a group to die by suicide.

They don't.

• An earthworm that is cut in half becomes two earthworms.

It doesn't. The head may grow a new back end, but the back end will die.

• The color red makes bulls aggressive.

It doesn't. Bulls are color-blind to red. They charge toward the matador because of the movement of the cape.

• Bats are blind.

They aren't. While they *do* bounce sound waves off their environment to help them fly around without hitting stuff, they have vision too.

• Koalas are bears.

They're not. Call them koala bears if you want, but they're marsupials.

• Goldfish have a three-second memory.

They don't. They can learn and remember things. Research at Plymouth University showed that goldfish have a memory span of up to three months.

● ● ● ●

Arlo, we really need to talk about the elephant in the room—elephants! Did you know that elephants can smell water up to twelve miles away?

 Water smells?

 It does to an elephant. And speaking of elephants, it's

time for . . .

Chapter 4

The Biggest and Smallest Animals

 Elephants are *big*. Duh, right? An elephant's trunk alone has around forty *thousand* muscles in it. Its teeth can be more than eight inches from front to back, and each tooth can weigh more than eight pounds. Its brain is nearly eleven pounds. I guess that's why elephants never forget.

The African elephant is the largest living land mammal, with the males weighing up to seven tons. They should go on Weight Watchers, if you ask me. It worked for my mom.

But the elephant is *not* the largest animal in the world. That would be the blue whale. It's almost a hundred feet long and can weigh two hundred *tons*. Its heart is the size of a small car! It could fit three school buses inside it! Some of its blood vessels are big enough to crawl through! That is, if you enjoy crawling through giant blood vessels. That sounds yucky to me.

 By the way, do you know why elephants look so wrinkled?*

---

*Because they don't fit on an ironing board

 The green anaconda is the world's largest snake. Found in South America, it can grow to be more than twenty-nine feet long and weigh over five hundred pounds.

 The largest reptile in the world is the salt-water crocodile. It can reach twenty feet long. You probably don't want to flush one of these guys down your toilet.

Giraffes are the tallest mammals in the world. They can

reach food nearly twenty feet off the ground.

 The southern elephant seal is the largest meat eater in the world. The males are usually five or six times heavier than the females—almost nine thousand pounds. I guess that's because they spend too much time sitting around watching football.

 Seals don't watch football games, Arlo!

They should. Watching foot-ball is cool. The Nomura's

jellyfish is found off the coasts of China and North and South Korea. One of them can weigh up to four hundred and forty pounds. That's about the same weight as a male lion.

 The ostrich is the largest bird in the world. The males can reach

up to nine feet tall and weigh almost three hundred and fifty pounds. Naturally, ostrich eggs are the largest bird eggs in the world. They can weigh three pounds each.

 The largest bat in the world is the giant golden-crowned flying fox, a fruit bat from the caves and rain forests of the Philippines. It has a wingspan of almost six feet.

Then there are the big *small* animals. The African giant snail can reach up to eight inches in length. That's big, for a snail.

The titan beetle is the world's

largest beetle, although I've heard that Ringo was pretty big. It can grow up to six and a half inches long and has a jaw so strong that it can break a wooden pencil in half.

 The goliath frog, from Africa, is the world's largest frog. That's not saying much. It's only a little more than a foot long. But it eats everything from fish and insects to other frogs.

 By the way, do you know what you call a girl with a frog on her head?*

---

*Lily

Now let's get *really* small. The bumblebee bat from Thailand is the smallest bat, about an inch long. It's about the same size as a bumblebee, so it has the perfect name.

The bee hummingbird lives in Cuba and is the smallest bird. It weighs about as much as a dime. It also lays the world's smallest eggs, which makes sense.

In the Amazon rain forest, pygmy marmoset monkeys are only about six inches tall. They're known as "pocket monkeys."

The *Paedocypris progenetica* is the world's smallest fish. It grows to about a third of an inch. It's found in Sumatra.

The *Brookesia micra* is the smallest chameleon. It lives in Madagascar and can fit on the head of a matchstick.

Thread snakes are the world's smallest snakes. They're less than four inches long.

The world's smallest tortoise is the speckled padloper from South Africa and southern Namibia. The adult males are just two or three inches long. Adult females are a little bigger.

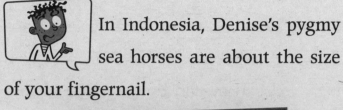 In Indonesia, Denise's pygmy sea horses are about the size of your fingernail.

Pygmy sea horse

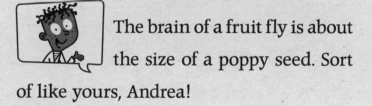 The brain of a fruit fly is about the size of a poppy seed. Sort of like yours, Andrea!

 I'm just going to ignore that.

Because I'm mature. Not like *some* people I know, Arlo. It just so happens that having a small brain doesn't mean the animal is dumb. Even insects can solve problems and learn things. Bumblebees have nearly a million brain cells. They can be taught to push a ball to the center of a platform to get a sugary treat. Honeybees do a little tail-shaking dance called "the waggle" to let other honeybees know where to find flowers that have tasty nectar.

 The smallest spiders, the *Patu digua*, are found in Colombia. They're about the size of the period at the end of the sentence that ends this chapter.

Chapter
5

The Fastest and
Slowest Animals

We human beings can go pretty fast when we're in cars, planes, trains, and rocket ships. But just using our legs, we're not all that fast. Some animals can beat us easily.

Horses are pretty fast. That's why they have horse racing.

But did you know that ostriches can run faster than horses? The maximum ostrich speed is about forty-five miles per hour. They can cover sixteen feet in a single stride.

When it goes into a dive to attack its prey, a peregrine falcon can fly two hundred miles per hour. How fast is that? In the 2016 Indianapolis 500 race, the winning car had an average speed of a hundred and sixty-six miles per hour.

The fastest sea animal is the sailfish, which can swim sixty-eight miles per hour. If my dad drove that fast on the highway, he'd get a ticket.

An average dog can run about nineteen miles per hour. But greyhounds can run forty-five miles per hour. They're the fastest dogs on Earth. Lions, gazelles, and elks can run really fast too. But the *fastest* land animal is the cheetah. A cheetah can go from zero to sixty miles per hour in just three strides. They can also stop really fast.

Did you ever hear the story of the tortoise and the hare? A brown hare is just a little thing, but it can run as fast as forty-seven miles per hour. That's way faster than the fastest human can run.* But the tortoise always manages to win the race by using its brains. So a slow-moving animal can be faster than a fast-moving animal. And speaking of slow animals . . .

If you look up "sloth" in the dictionary, the first definition is all about laziness. So sloths, which live in

_____

*About twenty-eight miles per hour

Central and South America, are really slow moving. In fact, they're the slowest-moving mammal. They take their time doing anything. How slow are they? When a sloth eats a leaf, it takes about a month to digest it. The three-toed sloth is so sedentary, algae can grow on its back!

Turtle racing is a thing! It works like this—a bunch of turtles are placed in the center of a circle about the size of a kitchen table. The first turtle to make it out of the circle is the winner. Can you imagine? People must like watching turtle races though. There's a giant turtle statue in Boissevain, Canada, to commemorate the old Canadian Turtle Derby. And Longville, Minnesota, calls itself the "Turtle Racing Capital of the World."

Speaking of lazy, how about cuckoo birds? They don't build a nest for their eggs. They just sit around and wait until *another* bird leaves its nest, and then the cuckoo will drop its own eggs there so the other bird will have to take care of them. That's not very nice.

You think *that's* lazy? After a giant clam picks a place to live, it doesn't move for the rest of its life. Sounds like my grandparents.

Sea horses are the slowest-moving fish. They are lousy swimmers. They move by using a tiny fin on their back that flutters up to thirty-five times per second. But they hardly get anywhere that way.

The Gila monster is a scary-sounding lizard that bites and  injects poison-ous venom into its victim. But don't worry. If one of them starts chasing you, just walk away. It can't catch up.

 Manatees are in no rush to get anywhere. Maybe that's why they're also known as "sea cows." Of course, manatees weigh over a thousand pounds. If I weighed that much, I'd have a tough time getting around too.

The American woodcock is the world's slowest bird. It only flies about five miles per hour. Sheesh, take your time, why don't you?

Nematodes are microscopic worms that feed on bacteria, fungi, and other nematodes. But they don't bother chasing bacteria around to eat. Nematodes are so slow they just wait for the bacteria to come to *them*.

But if you ask me, the slowest-moving animal in the history of the world is the garden snail. It moves at a top speed of about fifty yards an hour.

At the World Snail Racing Championships in England (yeah, that's a thing too), a snail named Archie covered the entire course (thirteen inches) in a blazing two minutes and twenty seconds. Wow! Archie left all the other snails in his dust.

Or in his slime anyway.

Chapter 6

The Smartest and Dumbest Animals

 Animals are smart! Take ants, for instance. They build entire cities where millions of them live. The cities have ventilation systems that bring air in and carbon dioxide and waste out. Some ants will collect leaves and take them to special chambers to decompose into fungus and be eaten by the ant

colony. No other animal besides humans does "farming" like this. It takes intelligence, planning, and teamwork.

 Oh, yeah? Well, I say animals are dumb. Ants can't read, can they?

Arlo, being able to read isn't the *only* way to judge the intelligence of an animal. Look at you. You can read, but you're not intelligent.

Oh, snap! In my face. Well, if you're so smart, smarty-pants, why don't you *prove* how smart animals are?

 I will! Orangutans can saw wood and use a hammer to nail boards together. They can even siphon liquids through a hose.

 Big deal. Any dumbhead can do that.

 Bottlenose dolphins are so smart, some scientists call them "nonhuman persons." They can recognize themselves in a mirror.

 Scientists can recognize themselves in a mirror?

 No! *Dolphins* can!

 Oh. So scientists *can't* recognize themselves in a mirror?

 You know what I'm trying to say, Arlo! Bottlenose dolphins understand when you point at something, the same way a dog does. They've learned how to hold a sponge in their beak so they don't get hurt foraging for food on the bottom of the ocean. In one experiment, it was found that a bottlenose dolphin would sometimes choose an "I'm not sure" option.

 That doesn't sound very smart

to me. If I ever took a test and wrote "I don't know" for an answer, I would probably get an F on the test.

Gorillas are smart enough to learn a version of American Sign Language. The most famous one, Koko, was able to learn more than a thousand signs and two thousand spoken words. In the 1980s, Koko asked for a cat, so she was given a stuffed cat. Koko didn't like it, so she was given a real cat, which she named All Ball. She cared for All Ball as

if it was her own baby. That must have been adorable.

Macaques are monkeys that have learned to use coins to buy vending machine snacks. In Japan, they've been observed making snowballs just for the fun of it.

Elephants are known for having emotions like people, especially when it comes to death and dying. When an elephant dies, other elephants will stay close to it for some time. They'll gather leaves, dirt, and branches to cover up the body. And if a herd of elephants comes across some elephant bones, they'll spend time examining them quietly. Sometimes they'll come back to visit grave sites of other elephants.

Crows are probably the smartest birds. They can be taught to speak, count, and even make knives to cut leaves and stalks of grass. Sometimes a crow will throw nuts on a road and then wait for a passing car to run over them and crack them open. Then they grab what's inside and eat it.

So you think it's smart to eat stuff that got run over by a car? I'll bet if I ate that stuff, everybody would say I was crazy.

African grey parrots are supposedly as smart as a four-year-old kid. The most famous one was Alex, who lived from 1976 to 2007. He knew lots of words, objects, colors, and shapes. He could understand the meaning of "bigger," "smaller," "same," and "different" too. Alex was so smart that when he was tired of being tested, he would say, "I'm going away now." And if his trainer looked annoyed, Alex would say, "I'm sorry."

Pigs can be trained just like dogs, and they also learn from watching one another. Mother pigs will sometimes sing to their piglets while they're nursing. I'd love to see that. Some pigs are good at video games, just like you are, Arlo.

 I would totally crush a pig if we played a video game together.

 Rats have powerful senses of smell and hearing, and some

can even detect land mines and bombs that we can't. They're also really good at figuring out patterns. It's no wonder why scientists like to put them into mazes to do learning experiments. One time, my family went to a corn maze around Halloween, and it took us hours to get out.

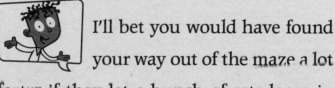 I'll bet you would have found your way out of the maze a lot faster if they let a bunch of rats loose in there.

An octopus can open a jar! It's true, Arlo. And if you don't believe me, have your parents YouTube it! You have to admit, that's pretty smart.

No it's not. Any dumbhead can open a jar.

 Have you ever had a raccoon get into your garbage, Arlo? They are amazing! No matter how carefully we humans design our garbage cans, the raccoons are smart enough to figure out how to get into them.

 Oh, yeah, well, if raccoons are so smart, how come they have to eat garbage? If they were *really* smart, they'd get their food at a supermarket. It would be cool if raccoons went to supermarkets.

People think of pigeons as pests. Well, maybe they wouldn't think that if they knew pigeons can recognize all twenty-six letters in the alphabet. Pigeons can also memorize complicated routes back to their homes after flying great distances. They can even tell the difference between paintings made by Picasso and paintings made by Monet. Can you do that, Arlo?

Paintings by *who*? But I *do* know that if I flew over a bunch of paintings, I'd be smart enough not to poop on them like a pigeon.

Arlo! No poop jokes! This book is supposed to be full of *serious* facts about animals.

Hey, you started it by talking about pigeons.

The *Portia labiata* jumping spider is probably the smartest bug in the world. To lure other spiders into its web, it will pluck out a rhythm at the corner of the web. Not only that, but it will remember the rhythm pattern to use the next time. That's smart!

So I rest my case. Animals are very intelligent, and sometimes they're even smarter than people.

Oh, yeah? Well, if animals are so smart, why don't they take over the world? I'll tell you why they don't. Because they're too dumb. Here, I'll prove it to you. . . .

Turkeys are so dopey that they'll just sit there and stare aimlessly at the sky for long periods of time, even when it's raining. Their eyes are spaced far apart, so they have a hard time focusing. This makes them tilt their heads to the side, so they look confused all the time.

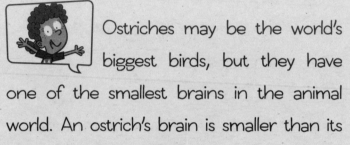 Ostriches may be the world's biggest birds, but they have one of the smallest brains in the animal world. An ostrich's brain is smaller than its

eyes. Sometimes when an ostrich is chasing prey or being chased by prey, it will start running around in circles because it doesn't know what else to do. What dummies!

Sponges are *really* dumb. What's their purpose in life anyway? To clean off kitchen counters? And starfish don't even *have* brains, so they can't be very smart. How about blobfish? What's up with them? They're just blobs of fish! So they may have the perfect name, but they're a bunch of dopes.

So in closing, I'd just like to reiterate* that animals are dumb. If they were smart, chickens would be eating people nuggets instead of the other way around. There would be people Parmesan and KFP—Kentucky Fried People. I rest my case.

 Let's just agree to disagree, Arlo.

 I disagree with that.

*That's a fancy word that means "say again."

Andrea's Top Ten Cutest Animals

Angora rabbit

African pygmy hedgehog

pygmy mouse lemur

pygmy marmoset monkey

harp seal

red panda

sea otter

teacup pig

meerkat

koala

Red panda

Chapter 7

Scary Animals!

I think Arlo and I can both agree on one thing—animals can be *dangerous*. Here are some animals that you wouldn't want to meet in a dark alley. Or *any* alley . . .

The cape buffalo, found in Africa, is about six feet tall and can weigh a ton. It will charge toward its prey at thirty-five miles per hour, and will even chase after cars and trucks.

So much for that African safari I was going to go on.

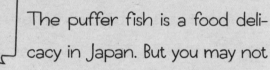

The puffer fish is a food delicacy in Japan. But you may not want to order one for dinner. If it's not cooked right, the puffer poison will paralyze your diaphragm and stop your breathing.

The good news is that if you eat a bad puffer fish and it kills you, somebody else will pick up the check for dinner.

Polar bears look cute and cud-dly in those TV commercials, right? Well, don't be fooled. They have no natural predators, and they'll eat just about anything—or anybody. I bet the only reason why polar bears don't kill many humans is because there aren't a lot of humans wandering around the North Pole.

 What about Santa and Mrs. Claus? They could get attacked

by polar bears! By the way, do you know why bears don't wear shoes?*

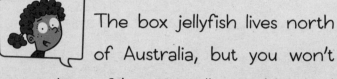 The box jellyfish lives north of Australia, but you won't see it there. It's practically invisible! And it has venom that's so powerful that human victims sometimes go into shock and drown or die of heart failure before they reach the beach. Box jellyfish kill more people than sharks and crocodiles combined.

 Remember those adorable lions in *The Lion King*? Well,

---

*Why bother? They'd still have *bear* feet.

in 1898, African lions killed more than a hundred people working on a railroad in Kenya.

Horned lizards can shoot a stream of blood out of their eyes to defend themselves.

I wish I could do that in case I ever get attacked.

 According to Guinness World Records, the Brazilian wandering spider is one of the most venomous spiders in the world.

 I hope they don't wander out of Brazil.

In 1957, some bees escaped from a Brazilian beekeeper who was trying to breed African honeybees with local honeybees. These Africanized honeybees spread through South and Central America, part of Mexico, and into sections of the United States. The "killer bees" swarm and chase their victims for a quarter mile.

Komodo dragons will eat anything, even humans. While they will swallow small prey whole, they stalk larger prey and then charge forward, rip out its throat, and wait while it bleeds to death.* But wait, there's good news too: Komodo dragons only tend to eat large prey once a month.

---

*Hey, that would make a good bedtime story!

The electric eel can deliver up to six hundred volts of electricity to anything—or anybody—who messes with it. That's enough to knock a full-grown horse off its feet.

Don't ever step on a driver ant. If you do, fifty million of its pals could swarm all over you. Great. That's all I need, to be attacked by ants.

I'd rather be attacked by ants than by a golden poison dart frog. It has enough poison in it to kill ten grown men.

In that case, I'm glad I'm not a

grown man yet. But I bet a golden poison dart frog wouldn't want to get into a fight with a blue-ringed octopus. It's only the size of a golf ball, but it has enough venom to kill twenty-six people.

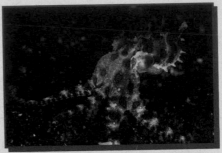

 I have good news and bad news, Arlo. The bad news is that the movie *Jaws* was based on a true story about a great white shark that attacked people at the beach.

What's the good news?

The good news is that sharks really aren't man-eaters. Humans are too bony, and after the first bite, a shark will usually leave you alone.

 Yeah, they leave you alone to *die*! And that's the *good* news? By the way, do you know where sharks come from?*

---

*_Fin_land

Saltwater crocodiles, which are found in India, Vietnam, and Australia, eat everything from water buffaloes to sharks. To kill its food, the crocodile flips the animal over and over until it drowns and falls apart. It's called the "death roll." I'm not sure I approve of all the violence in this chapter. It may be inappropriate for children.

 Hey, Andrea! What do you have against violins?

 Not violins, Arlo! Violence!

 I'm just yanking Andrea's

chain. Actually, the tsetse fly is probably the most dangerous animal. It gives people African sleeping sickness and is responsible for killing a quarter of a million people every year.

 But do you know what the most dangerous animal in the world is, Arlo?

 Gym teachers?

No, mosquitoes! Over one million people a year die from diseases that mosquito bites cause: malaria, encephalitis, yellow fever, dengue fever,

West Nile virus, and Zika virus disease.

Well, that's depressing. I hope the next chapter won't be such a bummer.

● ● ● ● ● ● ● ● ● ● ● ● ● ●

Fear of Animals

My best friend, Emily, is afraid of lots of animals. She has what is called zoophobia. A lot of people are afraid of specific animals. People who are afraid of spiders have arachnophobia. People who are afraid of horses have equinophobia. People who are afraid of bulls have taurophobia. Here are some other common animal phobias. . . .

Ailurophobia—fear of cats

Ichthyophobia—fear of fish

Cynophobia—fear of dogs

Ornithophobia—fear of birds

Alektorophobia—fear of chickens

Entomophobia—fear of insects

Apiphobia—fear of bees

Anatidaephobia—fear of ducks

Ranidaphobia—fear of frogs

Galeophobia—fear of sharks

Katsaridaphobia—fear of cockroaches

Spheksophobia—fear of wasps

Scoleciphobia—fear of worms

Myrmecophobia—fear of ants

Herpetophobia—fear of reptiles

Ophidiophobia—fear of snakes

Chapter 8

Famous Animals

 Cher Ami the Lifesaving Pigeon

It was in October of 1918, near the end of World War I. Over five hundred American soldiers were trapped in France behind enemy lines. They had no food or ammunition. They were being attacked by grenades, flamethrowers, and sniper fire.

They were desperate. So you know what they did? They sent out carrier pigeons with little canisters attached to their legs that had notes inside.

The Germans knew that carrier pigeons were great messengers, so they tried to shoot them out of the air. Two of the pigeons were killed, but one named Cher Ami (French for "dear friend") made it back to Allied headquarters twenty-five miles away.

At one point during his flight, Cher Ami was shot in the chest and fell to the ground. But he got up and continued his journey. When he arrived at headquarters, he was covered in blood and blind in one eye, and one of his legs was hanging on by its ligaments. But he completed his mission. As a result, Allied troops were able to save the lives of 194 soldiers.

Cher Ami lost his leg, but he was fitted with a wooden one and became a national hero. When he died the next year from his wounds, his body was preserved and is displayed in the Smithsonian Institution.

 Bobbie the Wonder Dog

In 1923, the Brazier family took a trip from Oregon to Indiana with Bobbie, their two-year-old Scotch collie.

At one point, Bobbie got lost. The family looked all over, but they couldn't find him. They drove back to Oregon, brokenhearted.

That would have been the end of the story, but six months later Bobbie showed up at the Braziers' doorstep in Oregon. He was skinny, dirty, and weak, and his feet were worn to the bone. He had walked over twenty-five hundred miles across the United States to get home!

Word got around, and Bobbie came to be called Bobbie the Wonder Dog. He was featured in newspaper articles, books, and movies. At a show in Portland, Oregon, forty thousand people showed up to see Bobbie. When he died a few years later, he was buried with honors at the Oregon Humane Society's pet cemetery in Portland.

 The Cat That Built a Dam
The Grand Coulee Dam in Washington State is one of the biggest electric power-producing plants in the world. But when it was being built in 1942, the engineers ran into a problem—they couldn't figure out how to run a cable through five hundred feet of a narrow, crooked drain pipe. No person could fit through it. No machine could move through it.

Then one of the engineers came up with an idea. A little white cat had been visiting the construction site for the past few days. Why not have the cat pull the cable through the pipe? So that's what happened. They tied string to the cat's tail and the cable to the string. Then they put the cat in the pipe, and the workers called to it from the other end. It made its way through the full length of the pipe, and when it came out the other side, the whole crew cheered.

Grand Coulee Dam

The only sad part of the story is that the cat's name and what happened to it afterward has been lost to history.

Smoky the World War II Dog

During World War II, an American soldier named William Wynne found a Yorkshire terrier puppy in a foxhole in the New Guinea jungle. It was tiny—just four pounds and seven inches tall. Wynne named the female terrier Smoky and carried her in his backpack.

For the next two years, Smoky served with Wynne in the South Pacific with the air force. She participated in twelve rescue missions. She survived a hundred and fifty air raids. She made it through a typhoon. Smoky even parachuted, using a parachute made just for her. On at least one occasion, Smoky used her keen sense of hearing to warn soldiers of incoming fire. Smoky was also the first war therapy dog.

At the end of the war, Smoky became a national celebrity. People would come to see her perform skills, such as walking a tightrope while blindfolded. Smoky lived until 1957.

Congo the Artistic Chimp

A number of animals have been known to draw and paint pictures. The greatest animal artist of them all was

Congo, a British chimpanzee. In the 1950s, he produced four hundred pieces of artwork. Famous artists such as Salvador Dalí and Pablo Picasso were big fans. Picasso even displayed one of Congo's paintings in his studio.

Congo was a temperamental artist. If he was working on a painting and somebody took it away before it was finished, Congo would throw a fit. And when he finished a piece of art and his human handlers encouraged him to keep working on it, Congo would refuse.

Congo was so popular that forty years after he died, three of his paintings were sold at an auction for more than twenty-five thousand dollars.

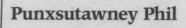

Punxsutawney Phil

Punxsutawney Phil is the groundhog who lives in Punxsutawney, Pennsylvania. Every year, just before sunrise on February 2, America waits breathlessly for Phil to come out of his burrow. If he sees his shadow, he has predicted there will be six more weeks of winter weather. If Phil doesn't see his shadow, it means that spring will come early. Phil has even been threatened with a lawsuit after his prediction turned out to be wrong!

It's all just silly nonsense, of course. Groundhogs can't predict the weather. But the town of Punxsutawney plays the whole thing up big, with guys in top hats and tuxedos. One of them holds a scroll that announces Phil's proclamation for the year. February 2 is celebrated as Groundhog Day all over the United States and Canada, and it has inspired a Hollywood movie and a Broadway show.

According to the Punxsutawney Groundhog Club, Phil was born in 1887, making him 123 years old, and his longevity is due to a special "groundhog punch," administered during the annual Groundhog Picnic. Believe what you want, but the average groundhog only lives about six years.

 **Heidi the Opossum**
In 2010, an abandoned

cross-eyed opossum from North Carolina was given to the Leipzig Zoo in Germany. Pictures of Heidi appeared online, and she became an internet sensation. She inspired a YouTube song and a line of stuffed animals, and she had more Facebook friends than German Chancellor Angela Merkel. In 2011, Heidi appeared on the *Jimmy Kimmel Live* TV show and predicted the winners in three Oscar categories.

Heidi the Opossum

TV and Movie Animals

As soon as there were movies, there were movies with animals in them. Film was silent in its early days, which was great for dogs and horses, which don't talk anyway, right?

The first animal movie star was a dog named Rover, the star of the 1905 film *Rescued by Rover.* It was about a baby who was rescued by Rover, so it had the perfect name. The movie cost just thirty-seven dollars to make, but it was so popular that Rover suddenly became one of the most popular dog names in the English-speaking world.

Since then, there have been hundreds of animal stars in movies and TV shows.

Here are a few of them, starting with dogs. . . .

Rin Tin Tin

An American soldier in France named Lee Duncan found this wounded German shepherd puppy during a battle in World War I. After the war, Duncan brought Rin Tin Tin home and trained him to do tricks. The dog got a movie role and ended up becoming a star in twenty-seven films.

In the 1920s, Rin Tin Tin was world famous. He got endorsement deals for dog food and signed his own contracts (with his paw print). He was the only dog in the Los Angeles phone book.

There were rumors that Rin Tin Tin got the most votes in 1929 and would have won an Oscar at the Academy Awards, but people thought it would look weird if a dog was named "best actor." Rin Tin Tin died in 1932 and was buried in France, where he was born.

Toto

She's adorable! In the 1939 film *The Wizard of Oz*, Dorothy's dog, Toto, was played by Terry, a female cairn terrier. She was owned by Carl Spitz, who ran a dog training school. Terry was a great actress with a special talent for sitting still, whether Judy Garland was singing "Somewhere over the Rainbow" or giant wind machines were blowing the air around to make it look like there was a tornado. Terry got paid more than the Munchkins!

By the time the movie was finished, everybody called Terry "Toto," so Spitz officially changed her name. Toto went on to make seven more films before she died in 1945.

Lassie

Lassie, a really famous dog character, was the star of eleven movies and three TV series from 1953 to 1999.

Over the years, there were lots of Lassies. Even though the character was a female dog, all the dog actors were male!

The first one was a collie named Pal. His babies Lassie Junior, Spook, Baby, Mire, and Hey Hey all played Lassie, and so did some of *their* offspring. In the end, ten generations of Pal's descendants have played Lassie. At one point, another collie was used, but there was such an outcry that the producers decided only a descendant of Pal could play Lassie.

Silver

Did you ever hear of *The Lone Ranger?* Me neither. But my grandparents tell me it was a really popular TV series in the 1950s. The Lone Ranger was a mysterious guy who wore a mask and spent his time chasing bad guys in the Old West with his trusty white horse, Silver, and his Native American friend Tonto. When the Lone Ranger shouted out, "Hi-Yo, Silver! Away!", you knew the bad guy's days were numbered. Silver was a real action hero.

There were actually two white stallions that played Silver. White Cloud didn't know many tricks, but he was really good at standing around and doing nothing while the Lone Ranger and Tonto were figuring out what to do next. For the riding scenes, they would switch to the other Silver, who was originally named Tarzan's White Banner and who was later renamed Hi-Yo Silver.

Mister Ed

Another famous horse was Mr. Ed, the star of a 1960s TV comedy series that had the perfect name: *Mr. Ed.* The interesting thing about him was that he could *talk.* I'm not kidding! Mr. Ed was played by a horse named Bamboo Harvester. He had a stunt double named Pumpkin.

Well, Mr. Ed didn't *really* talk. He just

moved his mouth and an actor would say his lines. They didn't have computer graphics in those days, so they couldn't just move the horse's mouth digitally. At first, they put a piece of nylon thread in Bamboo Harvester's mouth and pulled on it to make it look like he was talking. Ouch! After a while, Bamboo Harvester learned to move his lips when the trainer touched his hoof.

Flipper

There were a lot of weird TV shows back in the 1960s. Believe it or not, there was a show called *Flipper* about a dolphin that would save the lives of drowning people, "walk" on water backward, and even apprehend criminals! You'd think the criminals could just get out of the water to escape Flipper, right? Anyway, Flipper was played by five different female dolphins: Susie, Patty, Kathy, Scottie, and Squirt. A male dolphin named Clown was brought in for scenes involving the tail walk.

Gentle Ben

You would think it might be dangerous to put a 700-pound black bear in a TV show with human actors. Like, what if it got mad and decided to attack its costars? Well, *Gentle Ben* was the perfect name for the show because Bruno the bear was *really* gentle. (It also helped that he was declawed and his teeth were removed.) Bruno was so gentle that he'd let a man put one arm in his mouth without biting it. He was also good at making facial expressions and working with children. Bruno liked to ride an airboat on the show and devour lots of Coca-Colas and Tootsie Rolls.

Arnold Ziffel

If you think *that's* weird, wait until you hear about Arnold Ziffel the pig. He was one of many pigs to star in the 1960s TV series *Green Acres*. Most of the pigs were female, but the original was a male named Arnold.

Pigs are really smart, so the writers would have Arnold do lots of tricks and stunts. He could change channels on the TV, for example. He could also drink through a straw, play the piano, deliver newspapers, play cricket with a bat, and even carry his lunch box to school in his mouth. Now *that's* funny! In one episode, Arnold was drafted into the army.

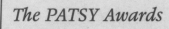 *The PATSY Awards*

In 1968 and 1969, Arnold Ziffel won the PATSY Award, which was given out every year to the best animal actors in movies and TV. It was sort of like the Oscars, but for animals.

This was no joke. In 1951, the first PATSY Awards were hosted by Ronald Reagan. That was before he became president of the United States and after he costarred with a chimp in a movie titled *Bedtime for Bonzo*. Lots of famous animals have won PATSYs— Lassie, Molly (who played Francis, the Talking Mule), Shaggy (from *The Shaggy Dog*), Spike (the dog from *Old Yeller*), and Flicka (the horse from *My Friend Flicka*).

The PATSYs were established by the American Humane Society. They were given out every year until 1986.

Hotel for Dogs

Dogs were so popular in Hollywood that they had their own hotel! Yes! From the 1930s to the 1960s, as many as seventy-five dog actors lived in the Hollywood Dog Training School in Los Angeles. It was on a nice ten-acre site, with a large grass playground, showers, bathtubs, electric dryers, and a full kitchen where dinners were cooked for the famous guests.

The Hollywood Dog Training School

still exists today, and it still has overnight guests. But they don't call it a hotel.

Presidential Pets

The presidents of the United States have always been surrounded by animals. And that's just their advisers! Herbert Hoover had a pair of alligators. Benjamin Harrison had two opossums. Woodrow Wilson had a herd of sheep. By the way, do you know how many sheep it takes to make a sweater?*

Martin Van Buren had a pair of tiger cubs. John Quincy Adams had an alligator that lived in a

---

*That's a dumb idea. Sheep can't knit.

bathtub in the White House's East Room. Thomas Jefferson had two grizzly bear cubs that were kept in a cage on the front lawn.

In the early days of our country, Washington, DC, didn't have a dairy or milk delivery company, so it wasn't unusual to see cows grazing in front of the White House. President Taft was our last president to have his own cow. He brought Mooly Wooly with him when he became president. When she died, Taft got another cow. Her name was Pauline Wayne. She was called the "Queen of the Capital Cows."

By the way, do you know why the cow crossed the road?*

 Andrew Jackson had Poll, a parrot he taught to swear. When Jackson died, Poll started shouting curse words and got kicked out of the funeral.

 When it comes to owning pets, the number-one president had to be Calvin Coolidge. He might as well have had a zoo at the White House! He had—take a deep

---

*To get to the *udder* side

President Calvin Coolidge with his dog Rob Roy, 1924

breath—twelve dogs, three canaries, a thrush, a goose, a mockingbird, two cats, two raccoons, a donkey, a bobcat, two lion cubs, a wallaby, a black bear, and a pygmy hippo named Billy.

 And hopefully, he had somebody to clean up after them.

 There's even an online Presidential Pet Museum. Have your parents Google it if you want to find out more information about presidential pets.

Chapter
9

Animals
in Space!

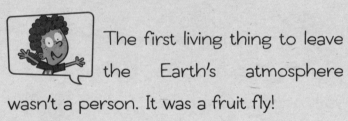

The first living thing to leave the Earth's atmosphere wasn't a person. It was a fruit fly!

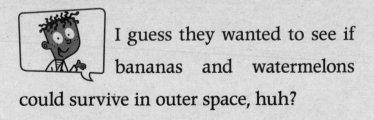

I guess they wanted to see if bananas and watermelons could survive in outer space, huh?

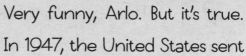

Very funny, Arlo. But it's true. In 1947, the United States sent a bunch of fruit flies into orbit. Since then, all *kinds* of animals have left the Earth so scientists could study how they would respond to this different environment: rats, rabbits, turtles, spiders, jellyfish, and algae. Here are a few others. . . .

Dogs and Cats in Space!

The first dog in space was Laika, a stray mixed breed the Soviets sent up in *Sputnik 2* to orbit the earth in 1957. She was also the first animal to *die* in space, because the Soviets didn't have any plan for her to return safely. That wasn't very nice.

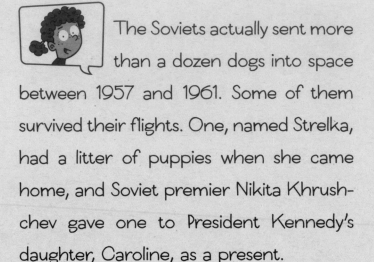

The Soviets actually sent more than a dozen dogs into space between 1957 and 1961. Some of them survived their flights. One, named Strelka, had a litter of puppies when she came home, and Soviet premier Nikita Khrushchev gave one to President Kennedy's daughter, Caroline, as a present.

The first cat in space was Félicette, also known as "Astrocat." She was launched by France in 1963 and returned home safely.

Chimps in Space!
To prepare for the first manned space flight, NASA sent up some

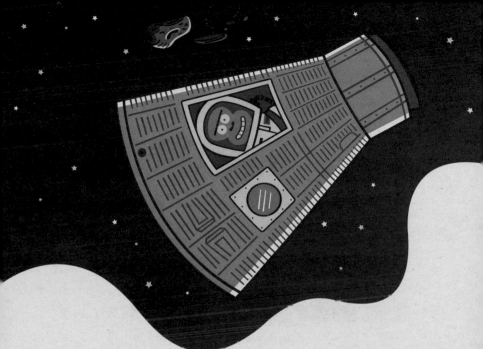

chimpanzees in 1961. Enos was the first chimp to orbit the earth. A chimp named Ham worked a series of levers, just as he had been trained to do. Both chimps survived their flights and landed safely. Ham retired after his mission and lived at the Washington Zoo until 1980. When he died, his remains were buried at the

International Space Hall of Fame in Alamogordo, New Mexico.

Enos prepares for his mission, 1961

Bugs in Space!

Before the space shuttle *Columbia* was launched in 2003, a high school student named Todd Nelson won a NASA contest when he designed an experiment to study how moths, bees, and flies would react in a weightless environment. Tragically, *Columbia* broke apart when it reentered Earth's atmosphere, killing seven astronauts. But amazingly, canisters with a bunch of nematodes inside were recovered from the wreckage, and a lot of the worms were still alive.

A jumping spider named Nefertiti lived on the International Space Station in 2012. Instead of spinning a web like most spiders do, she would just pounce on her prey. Since she couldn't "jump" in space, she adapted by sidling up next to her prey instead. When she got back to Earth, Nefertiti was put in the Insect Zoo at the Smithsonian Institution's National Museum of Natural History.

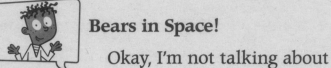

Bears in Space!

Okay, I'm not talking about *big* bears here. I'm talking about *water* bears. They're tiny, microscopic animals that are known for being able to survive just about any conditions. Water bears can live for years without drinking. They don't seem to care whether the temperature is broiling or below zero.

So in 2007, three thousand water bears were brought on the European Space Agency's Foton-M3 mission. Naturally, they survived.

Fish in Space!

In 2012, Japan sent a supply

ship to the International Space Station. It had an aquarium filled with medaka fish. The Japanese scientists found that instead of swimming in straight lines, the fish in space would swim around in loops.

By the way, do you know what part of a fish weighs the most?*

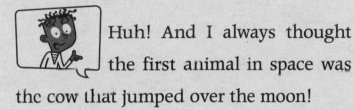 Huh! And I always thought the first animal in space was the cow that jumped over the moon!

---

*The scales

Chapter 10

Animals in LOVE!

 Oh gross! The L word! I think I'm gonna throw up!

 Love is an important part of the animal kingdom, Arlo! Animals fall in love with each other all the time.

 You said it *again*! Ugh, disgusting!

I don't need you around, you know, Arlo. I can just write this chapter about animals in love all by myself.

Go ahead! I don't want anything to do with that L word stuff. Good-bye!

Is he gone?

Oh goody. It's about time. I thought he'd *never* leave. Now I can talk all I want about love love love! I love love! What's not to love? It's so romantic, isn't it?

I think Adélie penguins are the most romantic of all the animals. They live in

Antarctica and gather together in colonies during the spring to find their true love.

When a male penguin finds a female penguin that he likes, do you know what he does? He pushes a stone over to her feet. Isn't that adorable? It's like he's giving her flowers!

Then, if the female penguin likes

him back, they sing a little song together. And after she lays her eggs, she and her true love take turns sitting on them to keep them safe and warm. I think I'm going to cry!

There are lots more animal love stories. The bowerbird lives in Australia and New Guinea. When a male bowerbird wants to attract a mate, he builds a fancy nest out of flowers, feathers, stones, and pieces of plastic and glass. That's true love!

The thing is, if he sees another male's fancy nest nearby, he might fly over there and wreck the place so a female bowerbird will come to *his* nest instead. That's not very nice! Boys can be so mean. I don't approve of such violent behavior. But I suppose humans also do a lot of weird things when they're in love. Why not animals?

The blue-footed booby is a seabird that lives in the Galápagos islands. When a male likes a female, he will raise up his big blue foot and put it down. Then he'll raise his other big blue foot and put it down. Apparently, that drives the girls crazy.

This probably is going to sound like a joke, but it's not. What do you get when you mate a male tiger and a female lion? A tigon! And when a male lion and female tiger mate, they make a liger.

Lots of bird species find a partner and stay together for the rest of their lives—ospreys, Atlantic puffins, scarlet macaws, and Canada geese. Others get divorced. About one out of four barn owl marriages ends in divorce. If the female doesn't lay enough eggs or some of their chicks don't survive, the couple will split up and the male usually keeps the nest.

 Can I say something about love?

 What?! Arlo, I thought you left.

 I did. Now I'm back.

 *And you want to say something*

about love? You, Arlo? Are you feeling okay?

 Oh yes. May I have the floor?

 Arlo, if you're going to talk about love, you can have the floor, the ceiling, and the walls.

 Okay, do you know how a male hippo attracts a female hippo?

 By pushing a stone up to her feet?

 No.

 By taking her out for a fancy dinner?

 No.

 By writing her love letters?

 No.

 I give up. How does a male

hippo attract a female hippo, Arlo?

 He pees and poops at the same time! And then he twirls his tail around like an airplane propeller and sprays his droppings all over the place! The female hippos are very impressed!

That's disgusting, Arlo! We said we weren't going to talk about that stuff!

 But it's a fact! So you have to live with it! Nah-nah-nah boo-boo on you!

 You're impossible, do you know that?

 Hey, you had your chapter to talk all about the L word. Well, now it's *my* turn. I get to write a chapter of my own. That's only fair.

Chapter
II
Disgusting Animals

Okay, let's be honest here. There's a reason why pigs are called pigs. They're pigs! Most animals are gross, if you ask me. Did you know that bats, parrots, earthworms, and orangutans eat dirt? Yuck! And get this— lobsters have little nozzles under their eyes, and to communicate with one another, they pee out of their faces! Really!

I'm not making this stuff up. Look it up if you don't believe me. Not only that, but wombat poop is cube shaped. And some pearlfish live inside the butts of sea cucumbers!

 That's it. I'm out of here, Arlo.

 Good. Andrea's gone. Now I can talk about some *really* gross animals.

Farting

First of all, let's talk about farting, shall we?

Like humans, many animals fart. It's part of life! When they digest their food, gases are produced. Those gases have to be released. And like humans, some animals release more gas than others.

When manatees want to swim up to the surface of the water, they hold in their farts. Then when they want to dive down below, they let out some gas. So  they actually swim by farting! Let's see you put *that* in your book report!

And if you think farting manatees are impressive, herring may *talk* to one another by farting! Scientists call them "Fast Repetitive Tick" sounds, or FRTs. Bubbles come out of the herring's rear end frequently. Based on when and where they do it, scientists* think the farts are a way the herring communicate with one another. But nobody knows what they're saying.

My guess is they're saying, "Who cut the cheese?"

Farting cows are not a big problem, but burping cows are! An average cow burps six hundred pints of methane a day. In fact, cows are responsible for about 4 percent of all greenhouse gases. So one of the ways to stop climate change would be to get cows to stop burping.

The world champion farter is the little termite. Eating wood must cause a lot of gas. Termites are responsible for *11* percent

---

* Scientists talk to each other by farting?

of all methane emissions. That's more than the amount produced by all the cars in the world.

As long as we're on the topic of fart- ing, let's talk about . . .

Smelly animals

Let's face it. Animals stink.* Hey, if *we* didn't use soap, we'd stink too, right? And some animals *really* stink. Here are some of the world's smelliest animals. . . .

The hoatzin is called the "stink bird" because of its putrid smell. It lives in the

*And animals that *used to* stink are extinct!

Amazon rain forest. And that's why I'm never taking a trip to the Amazon rain forest.

Hyenas roam around in packs, and they use smell sort of the way your mom or dad uses GPS to find their way around. They have pouches near their butt that produce an awful-smelling paste called "hyena butter." They rub it on stuff and even each other. Ugh, disgusting!

When animals are threatened, they don't just sit there and take it. Some of them fight back by stinking up the place! The zorilla, or striped polecat, shoots nasty stuff out of its butt glands that can be smelled half a mile away. Millipedes curl up into a spiral and release hydrogen cyanide gas. It not only smells horrible, but it can kill a mouse. Skunks spray nasty stuff called sulfuric thiols out of nipples attached to their anal glands. It contains the chemicals in raw onions that make you cry. The spray doesn't just stink. It also chokes your lungs and causes temporary blindness. The green wood hoopoe, a tropical bird in Africa, points its tail at threatening animals and shoots out dimethyl sulfide, the chemical that gives rotten eggs their lovely smell.

Do you know what vultures do to animals that attack them? They throw up on them! And because vultures eat smelly, rotting meat, their puke smells super-nasty. By the way, do you know what you should do if a vulture swallows your pen?*

Fulmars are gray-and-white seabirds that will eat anything, even garbage. When a baby fulmar feels threatened, it

*Use a pencil.

projectile vomits chunks of its stomach contents all over its attacker. That'll show 'em!

When male ring-tailed lemurs want to compete for females, they hold a "stink fight." Two lemurs will face each another. Then they pull their tails through the scent gland on their wrist and a gland on their shoulder that produces a gooey, long-lasting substance. After that, they flick their tail at the other male. Eventually, one of the lemurs can't stand it anymore and backs away. Some of these stink fights will last an hour.

On the other hand, there's one animal that smells *great*. It's the binturong, which is also known as a bearcat. It lives in

Southeast Asia. The binturong, they say, smells like buttered popcorn. Yum! Why doesn't McDonald's sell a McBinturong sandwich? I would eat that.

Binturong

Pooping

Finally, it's about time we talked about pooping, don't you think? I wanted to save the best for the end.

Get it? The end? Pooping?

Anyway, you know the beautiful white sandy beach you love to sink your toes into during the summer? Well, if you're near a coral reef, it may have been made out of parrotfish poop! It's true. The parrotfish grinds up chunks of coral with its big teeth to get at the algae inside. The rest of the coral passes through its digestive tract and ends up on the beach as sand. Enjoy your vacation!

A silver-spotted skipper caterpillar can shoot its poop five feet from its nest! That's sort of like one of us pooping across a tennis court.

Sloths only poop about once a week. But when they do, they poop *big*–about one-fifth of their body weight. A cow poops over a hundred pounds a *day*. It poops or pees once every twenty minutes or so. I'm guessing cows don't have to raise their hands to go to the bathroom.

Kopi Luwak is the world's most expensive coffee. Why? It comes from coffee beans that have been eaten and pooped out by an Indonesian catlike animal called the palm civet. The poops are collected and cleaned, and then the beans are roasted and sold for a price that adds up to more than six hundred dollars a pound.

What?! Coffee made from *poop*? To me, *regular* coffee tastes gross. They'd have to pay *me* six hundred bucks to drink coffee poop.

Okay, what I'm about to tell you next may be the single most disgusting thing in the history of the world. You may want to sit down for this fast fact. Are you ready? Okay, here goes.

Some animals eat their own poop.

Gross, right? I know. But it's true. There's even a name for it: autocoprophagy. Flies do it. Rabbits do it. Even educated gophers do it.

Why do they do it? Probably because they don't want to waste any food. By eating their own poop, they make sure that none of the nutrients in their undigested food get wasted. Hey, I don't like to waste food either. But you've got to draw the line *somewhere*.

Guinea pigs, chinchillas, lemmings, voles, and kangaroo rats all eat their own poop. In fact, guinea pigs will die if they *don't* do it. Dogs sometimes eat *other* dogs' poop. They'll even eat cat poop right out of a litter box. Ugh! I'm just glad Andrea isn't around to hear this stuff.

There was a time when toilets were commonly built up off the ground and pigs lived below them so they could eat the garbage and undigested human waste that dropped down below. And *that's* why they're called pigs.

By the way, do you know what you call a pig wearing earmuffs?*

Well, this has been an interesting discussion about poop, hasn't it? And by the way, if a grown-up or some uptight kid like Andrea tells you it's not nice to say "poop," just say "dung" instead. That's the first rule of being a kid. Dung and poop are the same thing, but it's perfectly okay to say "dung." Nobody knows why.

And that brings us to what I think is the coolest animal in the history of the world—the dung beetle. I mean, here's an animal that was actually *named* after poop!

The dung beetle loves poop. It lives in

*Whatever you want. It can't hear you.

poop. It lays *eggs* in poop. It rolls balls of poop long distances to provide food for its young!

Can you imagine being the son or daughter of a dung beetle? Your parents would come home from work and you'd ask, "What's for dinner?" And they would reply, "The same thing we have every night. Dung!"

Okay, now I think I'm even grossing *myself* out. And that's hard to do!

The Ending

 Okay, now you know *every-thing* there is to know about animals. You can go back to YouTube, junk food, and making armpit farts for the rest of your life.

 Wait a minute, Arlo! We didn't talk about endangered species.

We didn't talk about dinosaurs or any other extinct animals. We could do a whole book about that stuff! There are lots of other things to talk about too. We haven't even scratched the surface on the subject of animals yet.

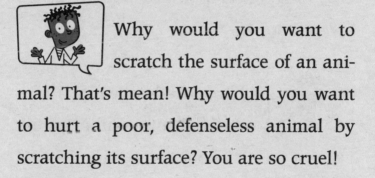

Why would you want to scratch the surface of an animal? That's mean! Why would you want to hurt a poor, defenseless animal by scratching its surface? You are so cruel!

Ignore Arlo. He's just trying to attract attention to himself. But I see we've run out of pages in this book. There's lots of information about animals waiting to be discovered by you. So poke around. Go online and search for the animals you read about in this book. Search for videos of them too. Animals are *really* interesting. Go to your local zoo or aquarium. You can also go to the library and take out other books about animals.

 Oh no! Andrea wrote the B word! Ugh, disgusting! I think I'm gonna die! Books are boring. Well, except for this one, of course.

 Oh, stop being silly, Arlo. You *know* you like to learn new things. You just won't admit it. Learning is cool. And the best part about learning is you get to impress grown-ups with how smart you are. I love doing that. Hey! Maybe one of the kids reading this book will grow up to be a famous scientist who studies animals.

Or a veterinarian.

Or a jockey.

Or a dog trainer.

Or you'll work at a zoo or an aquarium.

Or you'll become an artist who paints pictures of animals.

Maybe you'll grow up and save an endangered species.

Or wipe one out entirely!

But whatever you decide to do . . .

 It won't be easy! By the way, do you know what's black and white and red all over?*

---

*A sunburned penguin, a skunk with a rash, or a blushing zebra